VERSES *for*
MOM'S HEART

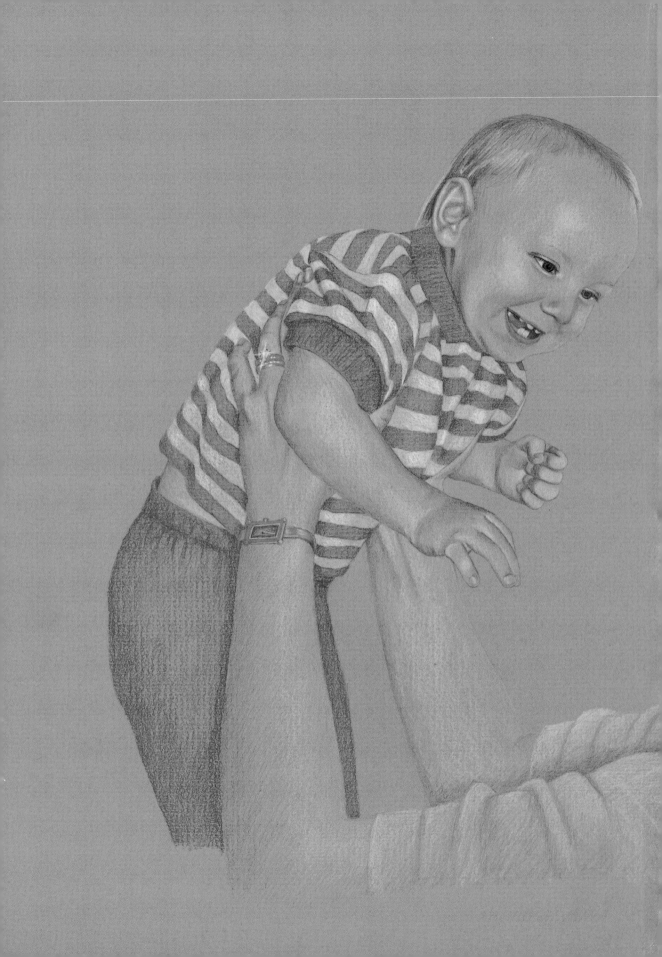

VERSES for MOM'S HEART

By Steven L. Layne

Illustrations by Gail Greaves Klinger

PELICAN PUBLISHING COMPANY
Gretna 2005

Text copyright © 2005
By Steven L. Layne

Illustrations copyright © 2005
By Gail Greaves Klinger

Library of Congress Cataloging-in-Publication Data

Layne, Steven L.
   Verses for mom's heart / by Steven L. Layne ; illustrated
by Gail Greaves Klinger.
      p. cm.
      ISBN-13: 978-1-58980-320-6 (alk. paper)
   1. Mother and child—Poetry. 2. Motherhood—Poetry.
3. Mothers—Poetry. I. Klinger, Gail Greaves. II. Title.
   PS3612.A96V473 2005
   811'.54—dc22
                        2005010178

Printed in Singapore
Published by Pelican Publishing Company, Inc.
1000 Burmaster Street, Gretna, Louisiana 70053

My Mother's Love

My mother's love
Has seen me through the best and worst of times.

When Sadie Abernathy laughed and said my ears were funny,
And I got picked last for kickball again,
And I forgot my *only* line in the second-grade pageant,

My mother's love enfolded me.

When I built a house of cards that stood for twelve minutes,
And I was elected sixth-grade class president,
And I put an airplane model together all by myself,

My mother's love celebrated with me.

When Danielle O'Connor broke my heart,
And I missed the basket that would have clinched the finals,
And our dog Tiger didn't wake up one morning,

My mother's love grieved with me.

They say that cries for *Mother*
Can be heard on the battlefield
Long after a war has ended.

And I ask you . . .

Is it any wonder?

Mommy's Work

"Mommy, juice!
Mommy, sleep!

"Mommy, books!
Mommy, sheep!

"Mommy, bath!
Mommy, ball!

"Mommy, shirt!
Mommy, doll!"

Bring it, find it,
See it, wind it.

Help me, show me,
Tell me, hold me.

From morning's dawn
To setting sun,

A mommy's work
Is never done.

I'm Tellin' Mom!

I'm tellin' Mom!
You broke my best toy.

I'm tellin' Mom!
You called me a boy.

I'm tellin' Mom!
'Cause you never share.

I'm tellin' Mom!
You pulled my hair.

I'm tellin' Mom!
You didn't clean your room.

I'm tellin' Mom!
She'll be home soon.

I'll stand in all my righteousness
And tell her all *you've* done.

I'll paint myself as royalty
And label you a bum.

I'll detail just how bad you are—
She'll blow up like a bomb!

[Sigh]

Oh, there's nothin' like tellin' you
That I'm tellin' Mom!

Lessons from the Master

Once when Mom was hurting,
I felt all squishy inside.
No one told me that moms cry sometimes.

I climbed into her lap
And clasped my arms around her neck.

Then I patted her back
And whispered that it would be okay—
Just like she does when I'm hurting.

She must have forgotten how well it works.

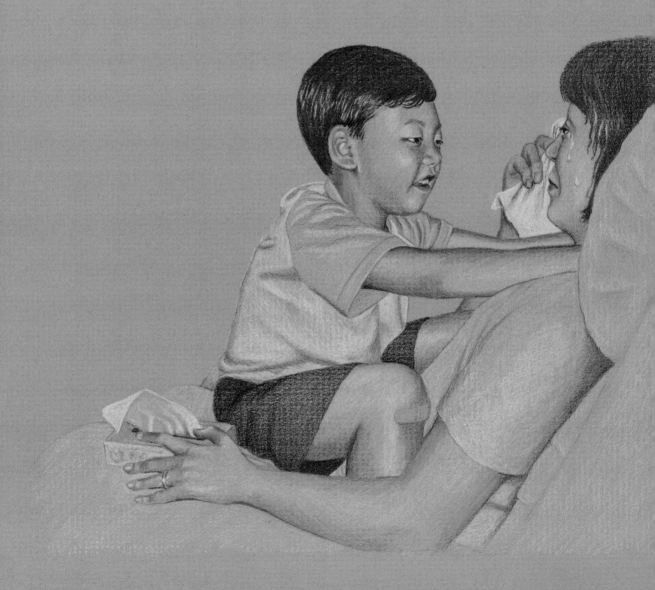

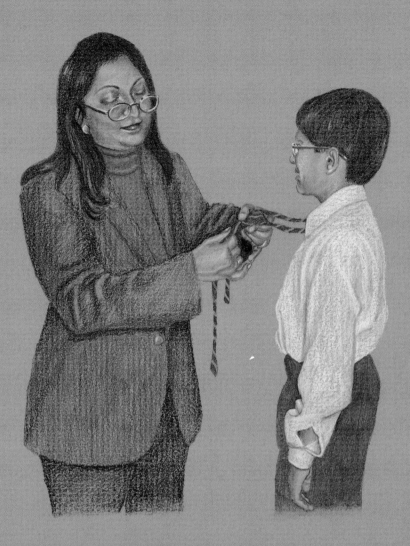

Momma's Boy

They said I was a *Momma's Boy,*
And they were surely right.

But if *their* moms were more like mine,
The world would be all right.

Note to God

Mom always tells us that even though
We didn't grow in her tummy,
We grew in her *heart;*

That God planned for us to be a family
Long before the world began;
And that our birthmothers were part of that plan, too.

We were talking it over the other day,
And we've decided that even though
Mom didn't grow in *our* tummies

(We're still trying to figure out where she *did* come from),

She must have been growing in *our* hearts all along
Because now she's ours forever.
And we wouldn't have it any other way.

Note to God: Nice work!

World's Best Mom

"My mom is the world's best mom!"
That's what I tell the other kids.

Suzie's mom jets all over the world on big airplanes.
My mom stays home.

Todd's mom works in a fancy office building in the city.
My mom stays home.

Brad's mom and Theresa's mom are starting their own business.
My mom stays home.

"My mom is the world's best mom!"
That's what I tell the other kids.

And when I come home from school every day,
And she's there waiting to throw her arms around me,

I'm sure I'm right.

The Best Story of All

Mom's the best storyteller ever.

In our kitchen, leaning forward on the table,
With warm cookies sending secret, scented messages,
We hear about the time she and her best friend
Tried to catch a hamster that escaped from its cage.

They both ended up on top of the couch screaming!

In the park, on our picnic blanket,
With autumn leaves playing tag in the wind,
We hear about how Grandpa belched so loud in church
That Preacher Baker dropped his Bible in the holy
waters of baptism.

People were still laughing when they came to church the
next Sunday.

In our family room, under a makeshift tent,
With lightning and thunder doing battle just outside,
We hear about her first date with Dad,
Their whirlwind courtship, and the fairy-tale wedding.

She wouldn't change a thing and neither would he.

Then Mom tells us a different story.
We've heard it before. Lots.

It's the one about the wife who loves her husband very,
very much
And how that love spreads to their children
And into the neighborhood and eventually out into
the world.

Mom tells that story *really* well,
Not only because she's the best storyteller ever,
But because our whole family agrees . . .

It's the best story of all.

Mom Deserves a Medal

Mom deserves a medal
For taking care of Dad.
Without her, boy, he'd be a mess;
His life would be so sad.

She packs his clothes for all his trips
And figures out his restaurant tips.
She does his laundry, cheers his teams,
Makes deposits, hears his dreams.

She runs his errands, makes his bed,
And stocks the fridge to keep him fed.
She irons his pants, ties his tie,
Hugs him tight to say goodbye.

Mom deserves a medal,
I certainly agree.
'Cause when she gets Dad straightened out . . .
She moves right on to me.

The Magician

When Dad's had a tough day,
He never asks for his favorite meal,
But it appears—*like magic*.

When Dad's gotta go away on a trip,
His suitcase gets packed with lots of stuff,
Folded all nice and neat—*like magic*.

When Dad forgets his sister's birthday
And doesn't have a card or a gift,
Something appears wrapped and ready—*like magic*.

When I ask Mom and Dad for an explanation,
Mom gets a twinkle in her eye.

"Love," she says, "is a *magical* thing."
Then she gives Dad a big kiss.

And I decide right then and there
That someday . . .

I want to marry a magician, too.

Teenage Drama Queen

I wish my dad would not call me
A teenage *Drama Queen*.
He doesn't get what life is like
For me at sweet sixteen.

My hair is wrong, my nails aren't long,
My lashes are the pits.
I'm way too tall, my breasts are small,
And can't he see these zits?

My friends all have the perfect life;
They're free of any stress or strife.
The hottest guys call on their phones;
They live in all the nicest homes.

Their sisters help them cook great meals
In size 6 dresses and 3-inch heels.
Their brothers always treat them right
And never once have picked a fight.

And *me?*
My life's beyond belief;
The cross I bear
Brings mounting grief.

Day after day,
I sojourn on,
But Dad insists
There's not much wrong.

It's Mom who listens to my woes.
Her eyes insist she truly knows
How bad it is, how sad things are
For girls who drive the *family* car.

She tells me she remembers well
Her role as *Drama Queen.*
How strange. It never crossed my mind
That Mom was once sixteen.

Firewalker

You *weren't* my mother.
I think I made that clear from day one—
I know that I meant to anyway.

Your presence in our house, *my* house,
Brought out a rainbow of emotions in me:

My face burned red, a scarlet stick of dynamite,
Every time you clasped my father's hand in yours;

My eyes glowed green, envy personified,
When my brother and sister hugged you with ease;

My heart froze blue, cold as ice,
The day you asked if I was feverish and dared to check.

I didn't want you.
I never asked for you.

> You
>   Weren't
>   Invited.

But still, you came,
Treading cautiously—just as you should have—

Never trying to be anything more than what you were.
Your peace offering was different for each of us.

Looking back, I see that for me
It was *time*.

You would have allowed my sullen silences to exist
Clear to infinity if that's how long it took.
I'm glad it didn't.

Of all the things I was *so sure* you were,
I never would have guessed . . .

You were a *firewalker*.

No Worries

Mom never worries
When she leaves us home alone.
She leaves her *in case of* instructions
Duct taped to the phone.

She's off without the slightest care
When we're unsupervised.
Her friends pop in on scheduled stops
To find we're still alive.

Mom has two extra cell phones
So a line is always free.
And she calls the house by *accident*
With sacred frequency.

The sitters must know CPR,
Be licensed in six states,
Avoid all body piercings,
And must rarely go on dates.

Our history of "home alone"
Assures her peace of mind.
The cops drive by half past each hour
With EMTs not far behind.

By next year she'll be so serene
When waving us goodbye.
It sure will be a *big* relief—
All *three* kids in senior high!

Refusals

You refused to rent a movie theater
For our birthday parties;
We made our own fun,
And it was always classic.

You refused to pay us
For work that contributed to our home;
We were given money
So that we could learn to spend, save, and be generous.

You refused to compare
Our grades and abilities;
We measured our performances
By old-fashioned effort and integrity.

You refused to shower us in praise
For being decent;
We followed the golden rule
Because it worked.

You refused to save us
From the consequences of our own poor decisions;
We knew forgiveness and a fresh start
Were available when needed.

You refused to question why
We didn't make the team, get the lead, or win first place;
We were encouraged to talk about how much it hurt,
and we were comforted.

No one ever refused to do so many things, Mom,
And accomplished so much.

Deep in Her Heart

Deep in her heart
There was room for a baby.
Deep in her heart
She was waiting for me.

Deep in her heart
She imagined and wondered
What kind of mommy
She'd turn out to be.

All through the years
As she guided and struggled,
Shaping the person
That I'd come to be,

She never forgot
How she'd longed for a baby.
Deep in her heart—
That's where *I'll* always be.

Decision Makers

When they needed someone to organize
The room parties in second grade,
I erupted with excitement,
"My mom will!"

And when they wanted an extra person
To drive for our field trip to the apple orchard,
I offered enthusiastically,
"My mom will!"

But when they needed chaperones
For the junior high school sock hop,
I shrieked with dread,
"My mom can't!"

And when they wanted a whole bunch of moms
To go with us on our eighth-grade trip to D.C.,
I explained apologetically,
"My mom can't."

When they needed someone to clean and press
Our band uniforms in under forty-eight hours,
I volunteered with confidence,
"My mom will!"

But when they wanted mothers to speak
At senior career day,
I proclaimed hurriedly,
"My mom can't."

Oh, but when the minister touched my hand and asked
Who would walk me down the aisle—
Now that Daddy had passed on . . .

My eyes overflowed with liquid sorrow,
And my lips surrendered to silence.

Then China-doll hands stirred and settled gently
On my shoulders,

While a voice spoke from behind me
With tender strength,
"Her mom will."

And my mom *did.*

Who would ever have guessed
She could be so decisive?

She must have learned it from me.

Secrets

When we were little
Mom kept secrets from us—

Like where she hid the birthday presents,
Who Santa *really* was,
And what our Halloween costumes would be each year.

When we were bigger
Mom still had her secrets—

Like where we were going on vacation,
How she always knew who did it,
And what *kind* of dog we were getting when she finally gave in.

Now that we're grown
Mom's secrets are still under lock and key—

Like Grandma's recipe for lemon bars,
How she can diagnose sick babies over the phone,
And where she and Dad got the money to take us all to Hawaii.

Mom's done a great job of keeping secrets over the years.

One thing, though, she made sure *never* to keep secret
Was how much she loved us.

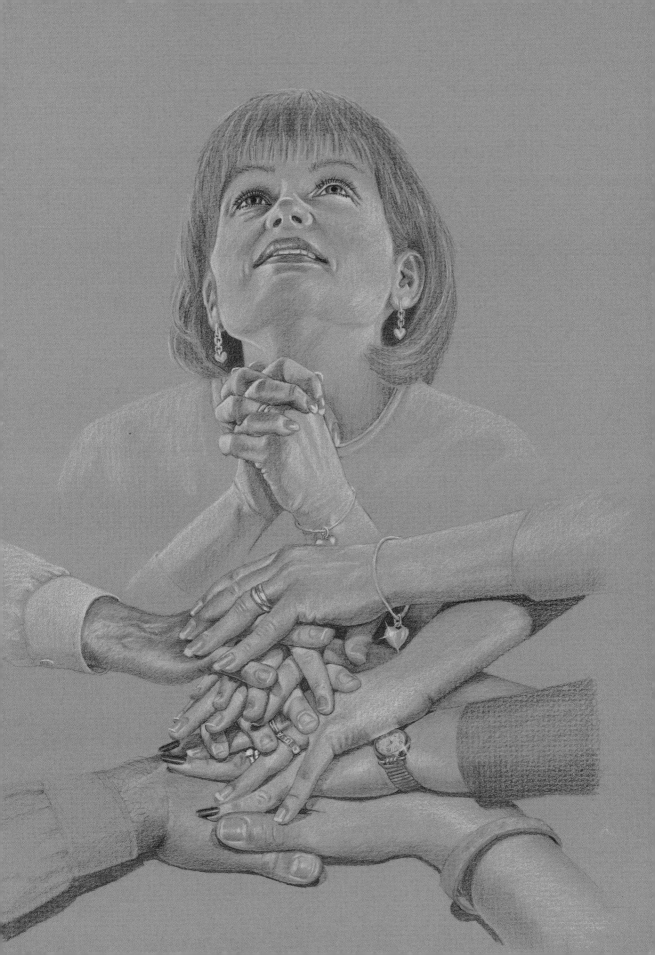

Everywhere

Up in the attic, opening your boxes
Of war letters,
Old Christmas cards,
And forgotten photos,

You're everywhere.

Out in the garden, handling your tools,
Uprooting stubborn weeds,
Raking back the soft earth,
And planting some lilacs,

You're everywhere.

Down in the kitchen, following your recipe,
Measuring the spices,
Layering the casserole,
And setting the timer,

You're everywhere.

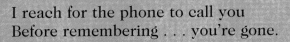

I reach for the phone to call you
Before remembering . . . you're gone.

What you've left behind
Is a legacy I couldn't understand before.

I understand now, though.
Now, I understand.

And I'm blessed today
And so thankful, Mom,
That even though you're gone,
You're still right here.

You're everywhere.

Legacy of Love

The last thing I was *ever* going to be . . .
Was *anything* like Mom.

When I was little
She kissed too much
And hugged too much and cared way too much
About everything that had anything to do with me.

When I got a little older, she was still a problem.
She planned special birthday dinners,
Taught me to write thank-you notes, and took me with her
To volunteer in the soup kitchen twice a week.

By the time I was a teenager, she was unbearable.
There was her passionate interest in my school life,
Her waiting up whenever I got to stay out late,
And her boundless joy over the graduation trip we took
together.

A college three thousand miles away couldn't keep her
down either.
There were her monthly care packages,
Her attendance at every parent weekend—four years in
a row—
And her having every breathing member of the family at
my graduation.

By the wedding, she was beyond help.
What kind of woman sells her car to pay for her daughter's wedding?
Crazy people do things like that.
Of course, I didn't find out until it was too late.

This last year, though, has been the worst.

The miles that separate her home from mine are vast.
She can't get around as well as she used to,
And I'm so busy keeping up with her three grandchildren
That it's hard for me to visit as often as I'd like.

I'm sitting outside tonight,
Listening to the crickets chirping just after dusk.
I've just put Carter, my youngest, to bed
With far more hugs and kisses than he wanted.

I'm planning my twelve-year-old Susan's
Special birthday dinner on a notepad
And writing thank-you notes to all the volunteers
Who work with me at the downtown soup kitchen.

I'm watching the clock because Kurt's curfew is up
In fifteen minutes, and he's still not home,
And then . . . the *strangest* thing happens.

I flip to a new page in the notepad and before I realize it,
I'm making a list of what I should put in the care packages
I'll have to send when he's away at college next year.

I walk inside, then, and over to the fireplace mantel.
I pick up my favorite photo of Mom in one trembling hand,
And my salty tears reveal an understanding that has evolved . . .
Quite slowly over time.

Tonight, though—
Tonight, it truly dawns and matures inside of me.
Because in my other hand, I am holding a photo
Of *my* precious children.

And the thought that *someday,*
I just might have to sell my car . . .
Well, that thought doesn't bother me one bit.

And it doesn't seem *nearly* so crazy to me.

Not anymore.